Make That Change!

Eight Steps for Crafting Your Ideal Life

Second Edition

K. DENISE DENNIS, PH.D.

Copyright © 2014, 2004 K. Denise Dennis, Ph.D.

All rights reserved.

ISBN: 1489596445
ISBN-13: 978-1489596444

DEDICATION

To my clients
- past, present, and future -
may you achieve your ideal life,
and more!

CONTENTS

Preface	i
Acknowledgements	iii
Introduction	1
Step 1: Envision Your Ideal Life	3
Step 2: Set S.M.A.R.T. Goals	15
Step 3: Form New Habits and Overcome Old Ones	25
Step 4: Calculate the Risks	37
Step 5: Chart the Path to Success	45
Step 6: Identify and Overcome Obstacles	59
Step 7: Find Your Motivation: Inside and Out	71
Step 8: Move Forward and Stay the Course	77
Review Your Progress	81
Epilogue	119
Appendix: Guide to Exercises	121
About the Author	123

PREFACE

I am often asked why I went into coaching. I didn't set out to be a coach. I was—and am—an educator. I began as a professor of management, teaching organizational behavior and management skills to M.B.A. students. Later, as public speaking opportunities arose, I formed my own training and consulting firm. In each training opportunity, participants would express interest in delving deeper into the matcrial. They enjoyed what they were learning about the topics: time management, leadership development, conflict resolution, networking, and so on, and wanted to discuss how to apply this material to their specific situations. The coaching grew from these post-workshop discussions. As I brought coaching into my business, I developed my coaching skills by attending a number of coach training programs.

Coaching is an excellent way to set and reach personal and professional goals; and yet, not everyone is ready—mentally or financially—to enter a coaching relationship. So, I have begun putting some of my coaching tools on paper so that everyone may benefit.

Enjoy!

K. Denise Dennis, Ph.D.
Prepared Mind Coaching, LLC

ACKNOWLEDGEMENTS

No success takes place in a vacuum. This work would not have been possible without the support of so many.

All great coaches have their own coaches, and I want to acknowledge all of the coaches I have worked with over the duration of this book project:

I'd also like to thank my fabulous photographer Herb Way, of Herb Way Photography.

Rebecca Williams did an outstanding job of editing multiple drafts of this book.

For ongoing support I thank my favorite tribe members: Andrea Woody and Deirdre Martin and, of course, my loving husband, Corlando.

INTRODUCTION

"Change will not come if we wait for some other person or some other time. We are the ones we've been waiting for. We are the change that we seek."

--Barack Obama

Welcome

Let me start by saying "Congratulations!" You have taken the first step in making positive changes in your life. In this program, you'll discover the eight steps to crafting your ideal life. Are you ready? It's time to Make That Change!

How to Use This Book

In this book, I will teach you how to craft your "ideal life." Read it all the way through. Then pick out the ideas that appeal to you, expand upon them to meet your needs, and start living the life you were meant to live!

While you can work at your own pace, I encourage you to tackle one step per week for eight weeks. I have included several exercises and spaces for you to record your ideas. Use the exercises to assist you in applying the ideas and concepts to your own life.

At the end of each chapter, you will find a "Reflection" page. Use this page to record your thoughts and feelings about the material you have read.

In addition, you'll meet two people who will be going through this adventure with you: Jeralyn and James. These fictitious characters are a compilation of my past clients, personal experience, and case studies. I have included them to give you examples of how the Make That Change! program can be effective in reaching professional goals (Jeralyn) and personal goals (James).

Use the Guide to Exercises checklist in the Appendix to record your progress as you work through the Make That Change! program.

STEP 1: ENVISION YOUR IDEAL LIFE

"The indispensable first step to getting the things you want out of life is this: decide what you want."

--Ben Stein

You picked up this book for a reason. You sense that something could be different, better than it is right now. That's a positive start! You are ready to make a change!

Your first step, even before we can talk about making changes, is to think about what you really want—or need—to change. Reflect on your life for a moment. Are you living the life you thought you'd be living? Are you "on track" with your goals? Are you living the life you were meant to live? How do you know for sure?

Let's begin with the end in mind. Who do you want to be? If your life were perfect—if you already had the job, family, house, lifestyle, interests, social life, physical state, financial status, and so forth that you have been daydreaming about—what would you be doing from day to day? This is an important first step—you need to have a clear idea of where you want to go with your life.

In the words of Henry David Thoreau, "Go confidently in the direction of your dreams. Live the life you have imagined." So, for today, begin with the vision of where you want to end up. Your first assignment is to take at least 30 minutes at some point today to write your ideal life statement (Exercise 1A).

Exercise 1A: My Ideal Life Statement

If your life were perfect, if you already had the job, family, house, lifestyle, interests, social life, physical state, financial status, etc., that you have been daydreaming about, what would you be doing from day to day? Take at least 30 minutes to write out your description of your "ideal life." I have included lots of space here; however, don't let the space limit you! Use additional paper if needed.

_____

_____

_____

_____

_____

_____

_____

_____

_____

_____

_____

ENVISION YOUR IDEAL LIFE

_____

_____

_____

_____

_____

_____

_____

_____

_____

_____

_____

_____

_____

_____

_____

_____

_____

_____

_____

_____

"You have to do what you love to do, not get stuck in that comfort zone of a regular job. Life is not a dress rehearsal. This is it."

--Lucinda Basset

Ideal life statements are powerful tools for clarifying your vision of the types of changes you want to make. If you don't believe me, just ask Jeralyn. Jeralyn started in the Make That Change! program because she wants to make changes in her professional life. She will be sharing her experiences as she goes through the program.

Jeralyn's Story

Jeralyn has worked in the technology industry for the past five years as a project manager. When asked to describe her ideal life, she envisions working in her own business as a software developer. She sees herself working from home the majority of the time. In her ideal life, "home" is a cabin on a lake in the Pocono Mountains, instead of the city apartment she currently rents. The more she writes down the details about living in her cabin in the mountains, the more she realizes that she would be alone for most of the day. While she likes the idea of working alone, she doesn't like the idea of total isolation. She adjusts her ideal life statement to include having a house in the suburbs where she can work from home, but will still hear the occasional car drive by.

One important lesson to learn from Jeralyn's story is the importance of not only writing out your ideal life statement, but also taking the time to think about what you have written. How do you feel about what is on the page before you? Once you get into the detailed description of your life, do you feel energized or drained by what you have written down? If you feel energized, great! If you feel drained, that is a sign that you'll need to make some adjustments.

I realize that your ideal life statement will never truly be "completed." You should revisit your statement on a regular basis to confirm that you are still committed to this particular vision

James will also be going through this program with you. He wants to make changes in his personal life. James will be sharing his experiences as well.

James's Story

James doesn't think he is assertive enough. He has a tendency to let people take advantage of him. For example, he doesn't complain when the waitress brings him the wrong meal, he keeps returning to the same barber who keeps giving him a haircut he really doesn't like, and he always loans his friends money even though he knows they will never pay it back. When James considers his ideal life, he thinks about living each day with the courage of his convictions. He sees himself asking for what he wants, speaking up for himself, and taking more responsibility for his own actions. After describing this ideal life, James states that he feels himself changing already—seeing it on paper is a commitment he is making to himself.

As James's example demonstrates, reflection is an important step in the change process. After you have completed your ideal life statement, use Exercise 1B to describe your reactions to what you have written.

Exercise 1B: Reactions to "My Ideal Life"

Review the Ideal Life Statement you created with Exercise 1A. How does it make you feel?

_____
_____
_____
_____
_____
_____
_____

Is this *your* ideal life, or the life others want you to lead?

_____
_____
_____
_____
_____
_____
_____

"Only I can change my life. No one can do it for me."
--Carol Burnett

How would your life be different if you were to have this life?

_____

_____

_____

_____

_____

_____

Is this ideal life something that you feel would be "nice" to have or something that you "must" have? Explain your response.

_____

_____

_____

_____

_____

_____

> *"A vision is not just a picture of what could be; it is an appeal to our better selves, a call to become something more."*
> *--Rosabeth Moss Kanter*

MAKE THAT CHANGE!

What will need to change in order for you to achieve this ideal life?

_____

_____

_____

_____

_____

_____

_____

Are you ready to commit to making this change? Why or why not?

_____

_____

_____

_____

_____

_____

_____

"Life is raw material. We are artisans. We can sculpt our existence into something beautiful, or debase it into ugliness. It's in our hands."
--Cathy Better

Now that you have a clear idea of where you are headed, I strongly encourage you to create a vision board as a visual reminder of your goals.

Exercise 1C: Create a Vision Board

To create a vision board, gather magazines and newspapers, and clip words, phrases and/or images that align with your ideal life. If your goal is to get in shape, find images of people who are physically fit. If your goal is to have your own home-based business, clip pictures of a person working at a computer in their home office. Use regular scissors or pick up a pair of fancy-edged scissors from a craft store.

Next, arrange the images in a collage. Some people prefer to create the collage on a standard 8 ½" by 11" sheet of printer paper. Others prefer larger poster boards. When selecting a board, consider where you will display it.

When attaching images to the board, I recommend using a glue stick. Glue sticks are easier to use and do not bleed through the paper the way regular white school glue can.

If you prefer an electronic vision board, consider creating a board in your word processing or presentation software program. You can collect images from online to add to your electronic vision board.

The most important thing to keep in mind is that you're not just creating a board, you should display your board somewhere where you will see it daily—on a wall, on your phone, on your computer desktop—the choice is yours!

Jeralyn's vision board is presented on the next page. Create your own vision board; then, use the "Reflection" page to note any additional thoughts and feelings about the chapter.

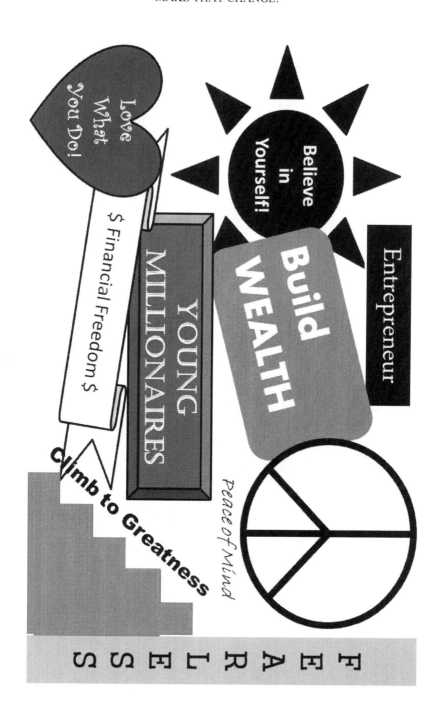

Reflections on Step 1: Envision Your Ideal Life

Use the space below to record your thoughts, feelings, and reflections about the work you completed for **Step 1: Describe Your Ideal Life.**

_____

_____

_____

_____

_____

_____

_____

_____

_____

_____

_____

_____

_____

_____

"People do not change with the times, they change the times."
--P.K. Shaw

STEP 2: SET S.M.A.R.T. GOALS

"If you want to get somewhere, you have to know where you want to go and how to get there. Then never, never, never give up."
--Norman Vincent Peale

What will it take for you to live your ideal life? If you are not "there" yet, you need to create a plan to take you from where you are to where you want to be. Setting goals is the next step in that direction. A goal is the end result of what you want to achieve after a period of time. Goals help you stay focused and motivated. When you don't have goals, you don't know which tasks are important and which tasks are "time wasters." Goals can—and should!—be personal and professional, long range and short range.

To make your goals even more effective, create what are commonly referred to as S.M.A.R.T. goals.

"S" stands for SPECIFIC:

Describe what you want to accomplish in as much detail as possible. When your goal is stated in specific terms, it provides clarity of purpose.

Jeralyn's Story

Initially, Jeralyn would simply say, "I want my own business." After realizing the power of stating a goal in specific terms, she now says, "I want to create a business that gives me the opportunity to use my strengths and display my talents while allowing me to create a sound financial future."

Write your goal in specific terms on the space provided on Exercise 2A.

"M" stands for MEASURABLE:

How will you know that you have accomplished your goal? What observable proof will you have when you are done? For instance, if your goal is to earn more money, you will know you have accomplished it when your paycheck displays a higher number. If your personal goal is to lose weight, you will know when you have reached your goal when you can fit into that pair of pants at the back of the closet. Indicate how you will measure your progress toward your goal on Exercise 2A.

"A" stands for ATTAINABLE:

Is this a goal you can actually accomplish? Challenging goals encourage us to stretch. But if we select goals that are obviously out of our reach, we are likely to give up.

James's Story

James wants to be more assertive in dealing with his barber—the one who gives the rotten haircuts. However, rather than starting out with a goal of demanding a refund of all of the money he has paid for horrible haircuts over the years, he begins by setting a goal of speaking to his barber about the type of cut he would like to have.

Turn again to Exercise 2A. Confirm, in writing, that your goal is attainable.

"R" stands for RELEVANT:

Be clear about why you are pursuing your goal. What makes this particular goal important? You will be more committed to accomplishing the goal if you are working toward something that you want to accomplish, rather than a goal forced upon you by your boss, significant other, or co-worker. Use Exercise 2A to indicate the relevance of your goal.

"T" stands for TIME-BOUND:

What is your deadline? How much time are you giving yourself to accomplish this goal? If you want to own your own business "someday," you may get it eventually, but you will move toward it more quickly if you say you will own your own business in two years. Also, consider when you will work toward your goal. Block out time in your schedule to make positive steps toward your goal each day. Even if that step is simply repeating your goal out loud--it's progress! Identify your deadline for accomplishing your goal on Exercise 2A.

When you have a clear idea about your goal, write it out as a single statement on Exercise 2B and post it someplace where you will see it every day. Soon, you'll be on your way to accomplishing your S.M.A.R.T. goal! Actually, I have allotted space for five S.M.A.R.T. goals on Exercise 2B. Feel free to continue writing your goals on additional sheets of paper.

Exercise 2A: Creating Your S.M.A.R.T. Goal

Use this exercise to word your goal in S.M.A.R.T. terms.

SPECIFIC: What do you want to accomplish?

_____

_____

_____

_____

_____

MEASURABLE: How will you measure your progress toward your goal?

_____

_____

_____

_____

_____

ATTAINABLE: How do you know that your goal is attainable?

_____

_____

_____

_____

_____

RELEVANT: What makes this goal important?

_____

_____

_____

_____

_____

TIME-BOUND: What is your deadline for achieving your goal?

_____

_____

_____

_____

_____

Exercise 2B: S.M.A.R.T. Goal Statements

Write S.M.A.R.T. goal statements outlining what you need to do to move closer to your ideal life, using the process detailed in Step 2. I've given you space to write down six goals, but don't stop there! Use additional paper to write S.M.A.R.T. goal statements for all of your personal and professional goals.

S.M.A.R.T. Goal #1

_____
_____
_____
_____
_____
_____
_____

S.M.A.R.T. Goal #2

_____
_____
_____
_____
_____
_____
_____

S.M.A.R.T. Goal #3

_____

_____

_____

_____

_____

_____

_____

_____

S.M.A.R.T. Goal #4

_____

_____

_____

_____

_____

_____

_____

_____

"Goals are dreams with deadlines."
--Diana Scharf Hunt

S.M.A.R.T. Goal #5

_____

_____

_____

_____

_____

_____

_____

S.M.A.R.T. Goal #6

_____

_____

_____

_____

_____

_____

_____

"It's never too late to be who you might have been."
--George Elliot

Reflections on Step 2: Set S.M.A.R.T. Goals

Use the space below to record your thoughts, feelings, and reflections about the work you completed for **Step 2: Set S.M.A.R.T. Goals.**

_____

_____

_____

_____

_____

_____

_____

_____

_____

_____

_____

_____

"If you don't know where you are going, you might wind up someplace else."

--Yogi Berra

STEP 3: FORM NEW HABITS AND OVERCOME OLD ONES

*"We are what we repeatedly do.
Excellence, then, is not an act, but a habit."*

--Aristotle

If only change were as easy as saying, "Okay—time for a change!" Instead, change is often a process of developing new habits and overcoming old ones. A habit is a repeated action that is usually done without thinking. Unfortunately, bad habits are like a comfortable bed, easy to get into, but hard to get out of. You can probably list your bad habits. Maybe you always have two servings of dessert—even though you're full. Perhaps you smoke, drink, or gossip too much. Maybe you're a procrastinator. Just for fun, list a few of your "bad habits" on Exercise 3A.

I'm sure you have several good habits as well—returning phone calls in a timely fashion, recycling, exercising three times a week, and so on. Again, list some of these "good habits" on Exercise 3A.

To create positive change, you will need to create new habits.

Think about your ideal life. What new habits will you need to form in order to make it a reality? Use Exercise 3A to list the new habits you would like to form.

Exercise 3A: Bad, Good, and New Habits

Take stock of your bad habits and good habits, and then list the new habits you would like to form.

List a few of your bad habits.

_____

_____

_____

_____

_____

List a few of your good habits.

_____

_____

_____

_____

_____

"Being willing to change allows you to move from a point of view to a viewing point—a higher, more expansive place, from which you can see both sides."

--Thomas Crum

List at least five new habits you will need to form in order to accomplish your goal(s).

1. _____

2. _____

3. _____

4. _____

5. _____

Habits are merely behaviors repeated again and again until they become second nature. To create new habits, you simply need to identify those new behaviors you need to repeat, and then commit to repeating them. This involves a combination of intention, environment, and effort.

Intention

First, clearly state why you want to create this new habit—this is your intention. Review your ideal life description if you need additional motivation. Your intention serves as a beacon; something on which to stay focused so you don't veer off course. Of course, it is best to state your intention in writing. The writing process helps to solidify your thoughts.

"If you are going to achieve excellence in big things, you develop the habit in little matters. Excellence is not an exception, it is a prevailing attitude."
--Colin Powell

Environment

Next, you need to create an environment that will support your new habit. If your intention is to lose weight, get rid of the junk food in your cabinets and replace it with healthy snacks. If your intention is to network more often, place business cards in all of your handbags.

James's Story

James belongs to a local gym, but besides paying his membership dues every month, he doesn't really go. He wants to create a new habit around going to the gym three times a week. His intention is clear—he wants to work out for 30 minutes every Monday, Wednesday, and Friday morning as soon as he wakes up. He creates a supportive environment by placing his gym bag next to his bed so that it is the first thing he sees when he wakes up in the morning. This increases the likelihood that James will make the effort to get to the gym. When the alarm clock rings in the morning, James is up and out the door!

Effort

Finally, you need to expend effort toward the new habit—in the words of a once popular shoe commercial, "Just Do It!"

The key to creating a new habit is to stick with it. Practice your new habit every chance you get. Don't be discouraged if you don't see immediate results. New habits take approximately three to four weeks to get established. If you can maintain your new behavior for at least this long, it will become part of your routine. Remember, you created the old habits—you can create the new ones, too!

If you need additional support, read books or listen to podcasts related to the subject you want to change. Learning how other people have successfully accomplished this goal can be helpful.

Also, look to your own past successes. Think about times in the past when you successfully stopped a bad habit or started a good one. How did you do it? What methods worked for you?

> **Jeralyn's Story**
>
> Jeralyn wants to develop a habit of starting conversations at networking functions. She has never felt comfortable speaking to people at events. To prepare, she states her intention: "I want to start conversations so I can make the connections that will grow my new business." She then sets up a supportive environment. She creates a list of ten "small talk" topics that she will use at the event. She also commits to moving away from the hors d' oeuvres. Normally, she stands next to the buffalo wings and chips, keeping her mouth full so she doesn't have to talk. At the next networking event she attends, she attempts to put forth the effort. She approaches a small group of people, but feels too uncomfortable to speak. Rather than become discouraged, she acknowledges that she made progress, and vows to try again at the next event.

Finally, and most importantly—if you do happen to fall back into the old routines, forgive yourself and try again.

Pause here and complete Exercise 3B, which focuses on one of the new habits you need to develop.

Exercise 3B: Forming New Habits

What is one new habit you will need to form in order to accomplish your goal?

_____

_____

_____

_____

_____

_____

Intention: Why is it important to form this particular habit?

_____

_____

_____

_____

_____

_____

"Character is long-standing habit."

--Plutarch

Environment: What changes will you need to make in your environment in order to accomplish this new habit?

_____

_____

_____

_____

_____

_____

Effort: When and how will you practice your new habit?

_____

_____

_____

_____

_____

_____

"Habits... the only reason they persist is that they are offering some satisfaction. You allow them to persist by not seeking any other, better form of satisfying the same needs. Every habit, good or bad, is acquired and learned in the same way – by finding that it is a means of satisfaction."
--Juliene Berk

In addition to forming new habits, you need to develop a strategy for overcoming the old unhealthy ones. It can be difficult to quit an old, comfortable, habit on the spot. Often it helps to use substitutions.

Jeralyn's Story

After working at her full-time job all day, Jeralyn usually plants herself on the couch as soon as she gets home and watches a few hours of television. She recognizes that this habit is not moving her closer to her ideal life, but night after night she finds herself on the couch again, flipping channels. After thinking about this habit, she realizes that her real need is to wind down after work. Jeralyn decides to replace her television habit with a new habit—listening to her favorite playlist for thirty minutes. This allows her to transition from her full-time work to the time she would like to devote to her business. After consciously implementing this substitution for a week, it became easier and easier for her to break the old television habit.

How could you apply this substitution technique to overcome a few of your old habits? Use Exercise 3C to record your thoughts.

"The best way to break a bad habit is to drop it."
--Leo Aikman

Exercise 3C: Overcoming Old Habits

Return to the list of bad habits you created in Exercise 3A. You may wish to focus on one or two of them for this exercise.

Old Habit #1:

What habit would you like to stop?
_____
_____

What role is this habit playing in your life? (Relaxation? Escape? Hunger? Emotional Release? Something else?)
_____
_____
_____

What new habit could you replace it with?
_____
_____

What would this substitution allow you to accomplish?
_____
_____
_____

Old Habit #2:

What habit would you like to stop?

_____

_____

What role is this habit playing in your life? (Relaxation? Escape? Hunger? Emotional Release? Something else?)

_____

_____

_____

_____

What new habit could you replace it with?

_____

_____

What would this substitution allow you to accomplish?

_____

_____

_____

_____

Reflections on Step 3: Form New Habits and Overcome Old Ones

Use the space below to record your thoughts, feelings, and reflections about the work you completed for **Step 3: Form New Habits and Overcome Old Ones**.

_____

_____

_____

_____

_____

_____

_____

_____

_____

_____

_____

_____

_____

_____

_____

"Any act often repeated soon forms a habit; and habit allowed, steady gains in strength. At first it may be but as a spider's web, easily broken through, but if not resisted it soon binds us with chains of steel."
--Tryon Edwards

STEP 4: CALCULATE THE RISKS

"When I dare to be powerful, to use my strength in the service of my vision, then it becomes less and less important whether I am afraid."
--Audre Lorde

Changing your habits can be risky business. It's costly to make a change. Will it be worth the effort? Here's an exercise to make sure that the goal you set is worth the risk. Think about a change you will need to make in order to accomplish your goal. What are the consequences of making that change? Consider both the positive and negative consequences. Next, consider the consequences of NOT making that change. What are positive and negative effects of remaining the way you are?

James's Story

James considered what would happen if he became more assertive. James said, "If I were more assertive with my barber I might get a decent haircut—that would be positive! Then I wouldn't be embarrassed when I walked into work the next day.

On the negative side, if I started asserting myself, my barber might get upset and throw me out of his shop—or he might give me an even worse haircut!"

What would happen if James didn't work on becoming more assertive? James said, "On the positive side, if I don't speak up, things would stay the same and my barber and I could continue to have friendly, non-confrontational, conversations. However, I know I wouldn't feel good about myself, and that would be the biggest negative consequence."

Once you look at the pros and cons of taking the risk of pursuing a goal, you can determine whether or not it is worth it. If you decide a goal is worth the risk, you will be more likely to stay committed to it during the hard times.

Jeralyn's Story

Jeralyn is still trying to decide whether or not to quit her job and devote all of her efforts to launching her business. She contemplates the positive and negative consequences of starting the business.

Positives:

- Creative control
- Set my own hours
- Earn what I am worth

Negatives:

- Only earn money when I have clients
- Limited social life in the early years

Then, she contemplates the positive and negative consequences of remaining in her current job.

Positives:

- Steady paycheck
- Maintain current standard of living
- Friendly co-workers

Negatives:

- Investing time into someone else's business
- Could be downsized
- Limited opportunity for promotion

After reviewing the positive and negative consequences, Jeralyn decides that starting the business is indeed worth the risk.

Use Exercise 4 to write down the consequences of making your change, and the consequences of staying the same. Remember to include positive and negative consequences for each. When you're done, review your list of pros and cons. Is your change worth the risk?

Exercise 4: Calculate the Risks

What would be the positive consequences of making your change?

_____
_____
_____
_____
_____
_____
_____

What would be the negative consequences of making your change?

_____
_____
_____
_____
_____
_____
_____

CALCULATE THE RISKS

What would be the positive consequences of remaining where you are?

_____
_____
_____
_____
_____
_____
_____

What would be the negative consequences of remaining where you are?

_____
_____
_____
_____
_____
_____
_____

"The person who risks nothing does nothing, has nothing, is nothing and becomes nothing. He may avoid suffering and sorrow, but he simply cannot learn and feel and change and grow and love and live."
--Leo Buscaglia

Now examine the positive and negative consequences of changing or remaining where you are.

Is it worth the risk to attempt your change?

☐ Yes, it is worth the risk to make this change.

☐ No, it is not worth the risk to make this change.

If you are satisfied with your decision, then this is indeed the right choice for you. If you are still not sure, consider the pros and cons again. Is there anything else you need to evaluate?

Reflections on Step 4: Calculate the Risks

Use the space below to record your thoughts, feelings, and reflections about the work you completed for **Step 4: Calculate the Risks.**

_____
_____
_____
_____
_____
_____
_____
_____
_____
_____
_____
_____
_____
_____

"And the trouble is, if you don't risk anything, you risk even more."
--Erica Jong

STEP 5: CHART THE PATH TO SUCCESS

"One day Alice came to a fork in the road and saw a Cheshire cat in a tree. Which road do I take? she asked.
Where do you want to go? was his response.
I don't know, Alice answered.
Then, said the cat, it doesn't matter."

--Lewis Carroll

Great! You have a goal, you know what habits you need to change, and you have decided that the change is worth the risk. Now that you know where you are headed, the next step is to figure out how you are going to get there.

Let's say your goal is to advance to regional district manager by the time you are 40. What do you need to do in the next year in order to accomplish that goal? What do you need to do in the next six months? The next 30 days? This week? Today? These details form the basis of your action plan.

An action is something done or accomplished. It involves movement toward your goal. Having a good heart—a good intention—is wonderful, and an important part of the process. But the bottom line is that you must act in order to make your goals a reality. Remember the old saying: You may have a heart of gold—but so does a hard-boiled egg! It's more than merely the thought that counts.

In order for your plan to be successful, you will need to stick to a few simple rules:

Rule #1: Write It Down!

The plan must be in writing. You will need to refer to it often as you make progress toward accomplishing your goals. You'll be writing out your action plan later in this chapter.

Rule #2: Identify the Actions

Identify the actions you will need to take in order to accomplish the goal. Let's suppose that your goal is to earn a bachelor's degree in journalism in the next four years. What actions will you need to take in order to accomplish this? Here are just a few: apply to college, seek financial aid, and develop successful study habits. If your goal is to start your own business, you first need to choose the type of business to start, save money, and write a business plan.

Creating a goal map is a great way to identify the actions necessary to achieve a goal. Begin by writing your goal in the middle of the circle on Exercise 5A. Draw a circle in the center and write your goal in the middle, like so:

Exercise 5A: Create Your Goal Map

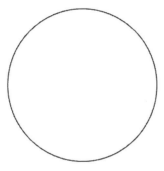

"Our goals can only be reached through a vehicle of a plan, in which we must fervently believe, and upon which we must vigorously act. There is no other route to success."

--Stephen A. Brennan

Then, ask yourself what it will take to accomplish this goal. Write each of these actions inside circles connected to the "goal circle." See the figure below. The elements in each of these circles are your "actions."

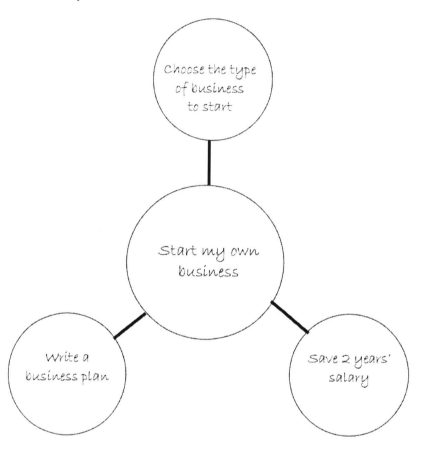

Rule #3: Control Your Own Destiny

The actions in the plan must be things over which you have control. Remember, you can't make anyone else change—you can only change yourself. Review the actions you included in your goal map. Do you have control over these actions?

James's Story

In the plan James first created, he stated that he wanted to make his co-worker stop shooting down his ideas. However, he has no control over his co-worker's actions. On the other hand, working on stating his ideas clearly and assertively is something he can do.

Rule #4: Set a Deadline

Indicate how you will know you have accomplished each action, and determine your deadline for accomplishing each step. Remember how a S.M.A.R.T. goal must be Measurable and Time-bound? Your actions must meet these criteria as well. When do you plan to accomplish each of the actions in your plan?

Jeralyn's Story

In order to build her software development business, Jeralyn wants to improve her networking skills. She decides she will know she has accomplished this when she sees that a minimum of 25% of her new business comes directly from new networking contacts, as opposed to advertising. She plans to reach this goal by December of this year.

Rule #5: Break Actions Into Tasks

For each action step, you will likely need to identify tasks that should be completed before you can achieve the action. For example, before she can begin networking, Jeralyn will want to create a separate e-mail account specifically for her new business and get new business cards.

Revisit your goal map. Now, create task circles off of the action circles, creating more details about the actions it will take to complete your goal. See the figure below for an example.

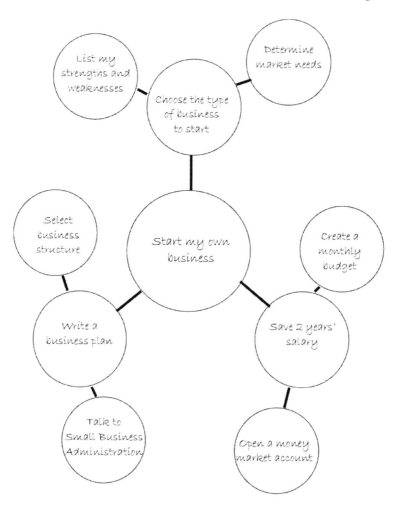

Rule #6: Prioritize Your Tasks

Wouldn't it be great if we could work on all of our tasks at the same time? Unfortunately, that's impossible. So, we have to make choices about what we will do first. Take care of the tasks that will do the most to advance our actions first. These are the "A" priority tasks. These tasks should be followed by the "B" and "C" priority tasks.

Goals are accomplished by completing actions. Actions are accomplished by completing tasks. Tasks are completed when you commit time to doing them! Now it's time to start using your to-do list, calendar, smart phone, daily index card, or other time management system. Ideally, you will spend your best time—that means both quantity and quality time—on goal-related tasks. Remember, these are your "A" tasks.

Pause here and create your action plan, using Exercise 5B.

Exercise 5B: Create Your Action Plan

Restate your goal (this is what you wrote in the center of your circle):

_____

_____

_____

_____

On the chart on the next page, list the actions you will need to take to complete this goal. Confirm that each action is under your control. Finally, indicate when you will complete each action.

MAKE THAT CHANGE!

Action	Under Your Control?	Deadline
1.	Yes/No	
2.	Yes/No	
3.	Yes/No	
4.	Yes/No	
5.	Yes/No	
6.	Yes/No	
7.	Yes/No	
8.	Yes/No	
9.	Yes/No	
10.	Yes/No	

For each action, list the tasks you will need to complete. Then, for each task, determine if it is a top priority (A), medium priority (B), or low priority (C). Finally, assign a deadline for each task.

Action 1:		
Deadline:		
Tasks	Priority	Deadline
1.	A B C	
2.	A B C	
3.	A B C	
4.	A B C	
5.	A B C	

Action 2:		
Deadline:		
Tasks	Priority	Deadline
1.	A B C	
2.	A B C	
3.	A B C	
4.	A B C	
5.	A B C	

Action 3:		
Deadline:		
Tasks	Priority	Deadline
1.	A B C	
2.	A B C	
3.	A B C	
4.	A B C	
5.	A B C	

Action 4:		
Deadline:		
Tasks	Priority	Deadline
1.	A B C	
2.	A B C	
3.	A B C	
4.	A B C	
5.	A B C	

Action 5:		
Deadline:		
Tasks	Priority	Deadline
1.	A B C	
2.	A B C	
3.	A B C	
4.	A B C	
5.	A B C	

Action 6:		
Deadline:		
Tasks	Priority	Deadline
1.	A B C	
2.	A B C	
3.	A B C	
4.	A B C	
5.	A B C	

*"Some people dream of success...
while others wake up and work hard at it."*

--Author Unknown

Action 7:		
Deadline:		
Tasks	Priority	Deadline
1.	A B C	
2.	A B C	
3.	A B C	
4.	A B C	
5.	A B C	

Action 8:		
Deadline:		
Tasks	Priority	Deadline
1.	A B C	
2.	A B C	
3.	A B C	
4.	A B C	
5.	A B C	

Action 9:		
Deadline:		
Tasks	Priority	Deadline
1.	A B C	
2.	A B C	
3.	A B C	
4.	A B C	
5.	A B C	

"Goals are dreams with deadlines."
--Diana Scharf Hunt

Action 10:		
Deadline:		
Tasks	Priority	Deadline
1.	A B C	
2.	A B C	
3.	A B C	
4.	A B C	
5.	A B C	

Commitment Statement (Complete the following):

I will make the actions and tasks in this plan my top priority because...

_____

_____

_____

_____

_____

_____

_____

_____

_____

"If you don't design your own life plan, chances are you'll fall into someone else's plan. And guess what they have planned for you? Not much."

--Jim Rohn

Reflections on Step 5: Chart the Path to Success

Use the space below to record your thoughts, feelings, and reflections about the work you completed for **Step 5: Chart the Path to Success.**

_____

_____

_____

_____

_____

_____

_____

_____

_____

_____

_____

_____

_____

"Whatever failures I have known, whatever errors I have committed, whatever follies I have witnessed in private and public life have been the consequence of action without thought."

--Bernard M. Baruch

STEP 6: IDENTIFY AND OVERCOME OBSTACLES

"Obstacles are those frightful things you see when you take your eyes off your goal."

--Henry Ford

Real and imagined obstacles can hinder our progress toward our goals. Those obstacles can come from within, or from those around us.

Internal Obstacles

Before we can make any other change, we must first change our minds. Often, we're our own worst enemy. Limiting beliefs keep us from trying anything new. A "limiting belief" is an idea that stops us from pursuing what we truly deserve. For example, if you hear yourself saying "People like me don't achieve that level of success," or "I don't deserve to be happy," you're probably falling victim to limiting beliefs. But limiting beliefs are just that: limiting.

People once believed the world was flat until Christopher Columbus proved it was round! People once believed that no one could fly faster than the speed of sound, until Chuck Yeager did it (in a plane, of course)! People once believed that it was impossible to run a mile in less than four minutes—in fact, doctors said that to even attempt to do so would kill you!—until Roger Bannister ran the mile in 3 minutes, 59.4 seconds! Are your inaccurate beliefs holding you back?

To see the effects of your limiting beliefs, first create a list of those beliefs. This is more difficult than it sounds - we don't usually view our own beliefs as limiting. Use Exercise 6A to assist you in examining your beliefs, feelings, and experiences about success, money, and happiness. One-by-one, review the items on your list. What proof do you have that these statements are true? Are they always true? Can you think of exceptions?

Exercise 6A: Identify Your Limiting Beliefs

Complete each of the following statements:

People like me are only successful when…		
Is this TRUE?	If so, is this ALWAYS true?	Is this belief LIMITING you?
Yes No	Yes No	Yes No

"Success is to be measured not so much by the position that one has reached in life as by the obstacles which he has overcome."
--Booker T. Washington

IDENTIFY AND OVERCOME OBSTACLES

Money is...

Is this TRUE?	If so, is this ALWAYS true?	Is this belief LIMITING you?
Yes No	Yes No	Yes No

I don't deserve...

Is this TRUE?	If so, is this ALWAYS true?	Is this belief LIMITING you?
Yes No	Yes No	Yes No

One way of overcoming those limiting beliefs is to write positive affirmations to combat them, for example: "I deserve success!" and "I welcome challenges!" Say your affirmations ten, twenty, one hundred times a day until you truly believe them. Use Exercise 6B to create one positive affirmation to combat your limiting beliefs.

James's Story

To aid in improving his ability to be assertive, James creates the following affirmation: "I am assertive. I state my position clearly and effectively." He writes it down on an index card and tapes it to his bathroom mirror, where he can see it every day.

Exercise 6B: Create Your Affirmation Statement

Develop a short, positive, statement that reinforces your goals and combats your limiting belief.

_____

_____

_____

Now, rewrite your affirmation statement ten times in the space allotted below or on a separate piece of paper:

1. _____

2. _____

3. _____

4. _____

IDENTIFY AND OVERCOME OBSTACLES

5. _____

_____

_____

6. _____

_____

_____

7. _____

_____

_____

8. _____

_____

_____

9. _____

_____

_____

10. _____

_____

_____

External Obstacles

In addition to internal obstacles, external obstacles can keep us from achieving our goals as well. In **Step 3: Form New Habits and Overcome Old Ones**, I discussed the role of creating an environment that supports your new habits. Your environment may also contain obstacles that must be overcome before you can make effective progress toward your goals. Take a good look at your environment—do you see any obstacles?

One common obstacle is disorganization and clutter. Before you can sit down at your desk and write your new business plan, you first have to find the desk! If you are a pack rat, with piles upon piles of papers, your first obstacle is to get organized. There are wonderful books on organization and clutter control. Or, if you don't have the time or inclination to do it yourself, consider hiring a professional organizer to work with you. Other environmental obstacles can be handled the same way.

Financial obstacles, such as the lack or mismanagement of money, can create a barrier to success as well. If you are struggling with your money, start making a change in that area today. Balance your checkbook. Open a savings account and make regular deposits. Make an appointment with a financial planner. Knowing your personal net worth will help you determine how much you need to grow—and in what direction.

You should also look at the *people* in your environment. Are they creating obstacles as well? Don't allow yourself to become a victim of O.P.D. - that stands for Other People's Drama!

"History has demonstrated that the most notable winners usually encountered heartbreaking obstacles before they triumphed. They won because they refused to become discouraged by their defeats."
--B. C. Forbes

IDENTIFY AND OVERCOME OBSTACLES

Jeralyn's Story

Jeralyn has had the dream of working as a software developer for years. She had even taken a few classes at a local community college. When she shared her dream with her best friend, the friend was quick to list all the people she knew in that field who had lost their jobs in the past five years. Jeralyn became discouraged and considered giving up her vision of her ideal life.

If your friends and family are not supportive of the changes you want to make, don't change your dream, change your environment.

Finally, recognize that you may not be able to overcome every obstacle. Examine your external obstacles and determine which ones can be conquered and which are real limitations. If an obstacle is a true limitation, do not be discouraged. Look for a different path to reach your goal.

For now, pause here and use Exercise 6C to identify external obstacles to your success and methods for overcoming them.

"Wanting something is not enough. You must hunger for it. Your motivation must be absolutely compelling in order to overcome the obstacles that will invariably come your way."

--Les Brown

Exercise 6C: Identify External Obstacles

What are the external obstacles that are preventing you from reaching your goals?

Obstacle #1:	
Can You Overcome This Obstacle?	
If YES, what will you do?	If NO, what will you do instead?

Obstacle #2:	
Can You Overcome This Obstacle?	
If YES, what will you do?	If NO, what will you do instead?

"It always seems impossible until it's done."
--Nelson Mandela

IDENTIFY AND OVERCOME OBSTACLES

Obstacle #3:	
Can You Overcome This Obstacle?	
If YES, what will you do?	If NO, what will you do instead?

Obstacle #4:	
Can You Overcome This Obstacle?	
If YES, what will you do?	If NO, what will you do instead?

"Our subconscious minds have no sense of humor, play no jokes and cannot tell the difference between reality and an imagined thought or image. What we continually think about eventually will manifest in our lives."

--Sidney Madwed

MAKE THAT CHANGE!

Obstacle #5:	
Can You Overcome This Obstacle?	
If YES, what will you do?	If NO, what will you do instead?

Obstacle #6:	
Can You Overcome This Obstacle?	
If YES, what will you do?	If NO, what will you do instead?

"It is only when we have the courage to face things exactly as they are without any self-deception or illusion that a light will develop out of events by which the path to success may be recognized."

--I Ching

Reflections on Step 6: Identify and Overcome Obstacles

Use the space below to record your thoughts, feelings, and reflections about the work you completed for **Step 6: Identify and Overcome Obstacles.**

_____

_____

_____

_____

_____

_____

_____

_____

_____

_____

_____

_____

_____

"Stand up to your obstacles and do something about them. You will find that they haven't half the strength you think they have."
--Norman Vincent Peale

STEP 7: FIND YOUR MOTIVATION: INSIDE AND OUT

"You must be the change you wish to see in the world."
—Mahatma Gandhi

As we have already discovered, change is hard work! It can take a lot to summon the strength to work on your new habits, achieve your new tasks, pursue your new actions, and act on your new goals. What can you do to stay motivated? There is not a single best solution. You must find the type of motivation that works best for you. Here are a few suggestions:

- Tape motivational and inspirational quotations around the house to help you maintain focus.

- Give yourself a small reward each time you make measurable progress toward your goal.

"Doing the best at this moment puts you in the best place for the next moment."
--Oprah Winfrey

Jeralyn's Story

Jeralyn brought a stack of 50 business cards to a networking event. She was determined to interact with people. She rewarded herself by promising to buy herself a movie ticket for every ten cards she passed out. At the end of the evening, she had distributed all her cards, earned five tickets, and had three offers for software projects.

- Follow in other people's footsteps. Seek out others who have accomplished the goals you want to achieve. Contact people you know or read the biographies of famous people that you admire. What can you learn from their experiences? How did they overcome the challenges they faced? How did they keep their eyes on the prize?

James's Story

James read biographies of people known for being assertive, including Donald Trump, Eleanor Roosevelt and Reginald Lewis. By following their examples, he learned that others would respect him more if he first had more respect for himself.

- Join with other goal-oriented people for mutual support. Look for groups specifically designed to support people making changes in their lives.

Consider gathering with groups of like-minded individuals on a weekly or monthly basis to share progress, good news, challenges, and successes. You can form a group on your own, or look for a coach who offers a group coaching program. I run group coaching sessions where my clients can hold themselves and one another accountable.

- Another alternative is to work with a professional life or business coach to craft a personalized accountability plan. Coaches help you set realistic goals and work through barriers to goal accomplishment. I conduct one-on-one coaching programs with clients around the world.

- A final tip is to act the part. Even if you don't feel like working on a habit, act like you do! Going through the motions will help instill the new behavior, even if you are not really motivated at the time. Eventually, your attitude will catch up with your actions.

Pause here and list at least five actions you can take to stay motivated on Exercise 7.

"Greatness is not in where we stand, but in what direction we are moving. We must sail sometimes with the wind and sometimes against it — but sail we must and not drift, nor lie at anchor.
--Oliver Wendell Holmes

Exercise 7: Motivation Strategies

What will you do to motivate yourself to work toward making your ideal life a reality? List at least five strategies:

1. _____

2. _____

3. _____

4. _____

5. _____

What will you do to create a support network of people who are committed to your success?
_____
_____
_____

> "Nothing will work unless you do."
> --Maya Angelou

Reflections on Step 7: Find Your Motivation: Inside and Out

Use the space below to record your thoughts, feelings, and reflections about the work you completed for **Step 7: Find Your Motivation: Inside and Out**.

_____

_____

_____

_____

_____

_____

_____

_____

_____

_____

_____

_____

_____

"People often say that motivation doesn't last. Well, neither does bathing – that's why we recommend it daily."

--Zig Ziglar

STEP 8: MOVE FORWARD AND STAY THE COURSE

> *"In this age, which believes that there is a short cut to everything, the greatest lesson to be learned is that the most difficult way is, in the long run, the easiest."*
>
> --Henry Miller

Congratulations! If you have followed Steps 1 through 7 of the program, you now have a detailed action plan for making positive changes in your life.

What you do next will determine whether your ideal life becomes a reality. You must use the plan! Treat it as a living document. Review it daily, weekly, monthly, and yearly.

Jeralyn's Story

A month after starting her plan, Jeralyn realized that she had progressed much faster than anticipated—she would be ready to change careers in six months rather than a year. She rewrote her plan to reflect her new deadlines.

As you begin to implement the plan, you will also discover areas that need more attention, and new areas for growth. You will find yourself rapidly growing, developing, and changing.

James's Story

James finally talked to his barber about his bad haircuts. His barber didn't particularly like the style either. He had been trying to make James happy! Together, they came up with a style that worked well for James. That first assertive step led James to seek other opportunities to improve his assertiveness. He revisited his plan and decided to work with a coach to help him determine the best way to reach his goal.

Are you on track? Are you making progress? Record your initial impressions on the "Reflections" page. Then, continue to track your development over the next year on the pages in the next section, called **Review Your Progress.**

Use your monthly and yearly review sessions to re-evaluate your ideal life description. Is this still the life you want to work toward? Have your ideals, values, desires, and/or needs changed? If so, don't despair, just follow this model and begin again. Benjamin Franklin said, "When you're finished changing, you're finished." We all change—for such is the nature of life. I wish you all the best as you Make That Change!

Reflections on Step 8: Move Forward and Stay the Course

Use the space below to record your thoughts, feelings, and reflections about the work you completed for **Step 8: Move Forward and Stay the Course.**

_____

_____

_____

_____

_____

_____

_____

_____

_____

_____

_____

_____

_____

"We can do anything we want to do if we stick to it long enough."
--Helen Keller

REVIEW YOUR PROGRESS

"Without reflection, we go blindly on our way, creating more unintended consequences, and failing to achieve anything useful."
--Margaret J. Wheatley

In this section, I have included weekly, monthly, and year-end pages for you to record your progress on your plan.

I encourage you to evaluate your progress on a weekly basis for at least the first two months. After that, check in with yourself at the end of each subsequent month. Ask yourself if you are still on track, look for potential obstacles, and identify any additional support you might need along the way.

Remember, it is in your day-to-day choices that the plan comes together. Prepare yourself, take action, and Make That Change!

Progress Chart Instructions

Months 1 and 2

For the first two months after starting the program, complete a weekly report on what you have accomplished, what worked and what you might need to change in the week to come.

Months 3 – 12

For the next ten months (months 3 – 12), review your progress at the end of each month. Are you still on track? Have your priorities shifted? Are there new obstacles to overcome? Identify your successes and challenges and reaffirm your commitment to your goal.

Progress Report: Month 1/Week 1

Date: _____

Are you making progress toward your goal? What is going well? What have you accomplished? What adjustments do you need to make?

_____

_____

_____

_____

_____

_____

_____

_____

_____

_____

_____

_____

_____

_____

MAKE THAT CHANGE!

Progress Report: Month 1/Week 2

Date: _____

Are you making progress toward your goal? What is going well? What have you accomplished? What adjustments do you need to make?

_____
_____
_____
_____
_____
_____
_____
_____
_____
_____
_____
_____
_____
_____

MAKE THAT CHANGE!

Progress Report: Month 1/Week 3

Date: _____

Are you making progress toward your goal? What is going well? What have you accomplished? What adjustments do you need to make?

_____
_____
_____
_____
_____
_____
_____
_____
_____
_____
_____
_____
_____
_____

MAKE THAT CHANGE!

Progress Report: Month 1/Week 4

Date: _____

Are you making progress toward your goal? What is going well? What have you accomplished? What adjustments do you need to make?

_____
_____
_____
_____
_____
_____
_____
_____
_____
_____
_____
_____
_____
_____

MAKE THAT CHANGE!

Progress Report: Month 2/Week 1

Date: _____

Are you making progress toward your goal? What is going well? What have you accomplished? What adjustments do you need to make?

_____
_____
_____
_____
_____
_____
_____
_____
_____
_____
_____
_____
_____

MAKE THAT CHANGE!

Progress Report: Month 2/Week 2

Date: _____

Are you making progress toward your goal? What is going well? What have you accomplished? What adjustments do you need to make?

_____
_____
_____
_____
_____
_____
_____
_____
_____
_____
_____
_____
_____

MAKE THAT CHANGE!

Progress Report: Month 2/Week 3

Date: _____

Are you making progress toward your goal? What is going well? What have you accomplished? What adjustments do you need to make?

_____
_____
_____
_____
_____
_____
_____
_____
_____
_____
_____
_____
_____
_____

MAKE THAT CHANGE!

Progress Report: Month 2/Week 4

Date: _____

Are you making progress toward your goal? What is going well? What have you accomplished? What adjustments do you need to make?

_____
_____
_____
_____
_____
_____
_____
_____
_____
_____
_____
_____
_____

MAKE THAT CHANGE!

Progress Report: Month 3

Date: _____

Are you making progress toward your goal? What is going well? What have you accomplished? What adjustments do you need to make?

_____

_____

_____

_____

_____

_____

_____

_____

_____

_____

_____

_____

_____

MAKE THAT CHANGE!

Progress Report: Month 4

Date: _____

Are you making progress toward your goal? What is going well? What have you accomplished? What adjustments do you need to make?

_____
_____
_____
_____
_____
_____
_____
_____
_____
_____
_____
_____
_____

MAKE THAT CHANGE!

Progress Report: Month 5

Date: _____

Are you making progress toward your goal? What is going well? What have you accomplished? What adjustments do you need to make?

_____
_____
_____
_____
_____
_____
_____
_____
_____
_____
_____
_____
_____
_____

MAKE THAT CHANGE!

Progress Report: Month 6

Date: _____

Are you making progress toward your goal? What is going well? What have you accomplished? What adjustments do you need to make?

_____

_____

_____

_____

_____

_____

_____

_____

_____

_____

_____

_____

_____

MAKE THAT CHANGE!

Progress Report: Month 7

Date: _____

Are you making progress toward your goal? What is going well? What have you accomplished? What adjustments do you need to make?

_____

_____

_____

_____

_____

_____

_____

_____

_____

_____

_____

_____

MAKE THAT CHANGE!

Progress Report: Month 8

Date: _____

Are you making progress toward your goal? What is going well? What have you accomplished? What adjustments do you need to make?

_____

_____

_____

_____

_____

_____

_____

_____

_____

_____

_____

_____

_____

MAKE THAT CHANGE!

Progress Report: Month 9

Date: _____

Are you making progress toward your goal? What is going well? What have you accomplished? What adjustments do you need to make?

_____
_____
_____
_____
_____
_____
_____
_____
_____
_____
_____
_____
_____

MAKE THAT CHANGE!

Progress Report: Month 10

Date: _____

Are you making progress toward your goal? What is going well? What have you accomplished? What adjustments do you need to make?

_____

_____

_____

_____

_____

_____

_____

_____

_____

_____

_____

_____

_____

MAKE THAT CHANGE!

Progress Report: Month 11

Date: _____

Are you making progress toward your goal? What is going well? What have you accomplished? What adjustments do you need to make?

_____
_____
_____
_____
_____
_____
_____
_____
_____
_____
_____
_____
_____
_____
_____

MAKE THAT CHANGE!

Progress Report: Month 12/Year 1

Date: _____

Are you making progress toward your goal? What is going well? What have you accomplished? What adjustments do you need to make?

_____

_____

_____

_____

_____

_____

_____

_____

_____

_____

_____

_____

_____

MAKE THAT CHANGE!

EPILOGUE

I hope you have enjoyed this program. It represents a labor of love. As I mentioned in **Step 8: Move Forward and Stay the Course**, the value in the program is not in the reading, it is in the doing. I encourage you to make a commitment to creating lasting positive changes in your personal and professional life.

If you need extra help, I encourage you to visit my website at www.preparedmindcoaching.com for additional resources. If you would like personal assistance in reaching your goal, I invite you to speak with me about coaching. You can contact me through the website as well.

I wish you all the best!

K. Denise Dennis, Ph.D.
Prepared Mind Coaching, LLC

APPENDIX: GUIDE TO EXERCISES

Use this chart to track your progress as you work your way through the "Make That Change!" program.

☑	Exercise Number and Name	
☐	1A	My Ideal Life Statement
☐	1B	Reactions to "My Ideal Life"
☐	1C	Create a Vision Board
☐	2A	Creating Your S.M.A.R.T. Goal
☐	2B	S.M.A.R.T. Goal Statements
☐	3A	Bad, Good, and New Habits
☐	3B	Forming New Habits
☐	3C	Overcoming Old Habits
☐	4	Calculate the Risks
☐	5A	Create Your Goal Map
☐	5B	Create Your Action Plan
☐	6A	Identify Your Limiting Beliefs
☐	6B	Create Your Affirmation Statement
☐	6C	Identify External Obstacles
☐	7	Motivation Strategies
☐		Weekly/Monthly/Yearly Progress Reports

ABOUT THE AUTHOR

For over twenty years, K. Denise Dennis, Ph.D. has been an educator, a trainer, a consultant and a coach.

She knows that coaching works! In fact, in her own research, she compared training alone to coaching combined with training. She found that management training increased productivity by 22.4%, while training combined with coaching increased productivity by 88%.[1] This study is often cited throughout the coaching profession.

Dr. Dennis earned her Ph.D. in industrial/organizational psychology from North Carolina State University. A lifelong learner, she has maintained her coaching skills by pursuing certification from the Career Coach Institute, Corporate Coach University and the International Coach Academy.

She has conducted workshops and training programs for numerous corporations, educational institutions, and non-profit agencies. Her coaching clients include entrepreneurs, professionals, and job seekers. In addition to her coaching business, she is a full-time faculty member at Bloomfield College (a private liberal arts college in New Jersey).

She currently resides in New Jersey with her loving husband and four rambunctious dogs.

For more information, contact
www.preparedmindcoaching.com

---

[1] This study was published under K. Denise Dennis's maiden name, "Bane." Olivero, Bane, & Kopelman, (1997).. "Executive coaching as a transfer of training tool: Effects on productivity in a public agency. *Public Personnel Management, 26*(4), 461-470.

Made in the USA
Charleston, SC
28 December 2014